Alcoholic or Problem Drinker?

The Difference May Surprise You

by Anonymous Guest

Legal Disclaimers and Notices

Alcoholic or Problem Drinker?

Table of Contents

Dedication

I want to dedicate this book primarily to the people of AA who inspired me so deeply over the last 38 years. My 3 mentors, (to date) who went to any length to help me, and to those who lost their lives to this disease. There have been far too many deaths due to alcoholism. I have learned valuable lessons from both of these types of people. Problem drinkers and those who have the disease of alcoholism. I'll discuss the differences in the following pages.

In the spirit of Tradition 7, proceeds from this book will be donated to AA and its supporting organizations.

Since Alcoholics Anonymous is an anonymous program and has a tradition of anonymity at the public level, I cannot identify my personal information, so I'll sign my name as,

Anonymous Guest

Preface

After all this time in the program of Alcoholics
Anonymous I've realized the need for a book that
the public can read, to learn more about alcoholism
and problem or addicted drinking. It took almost
eight years in Alcoholics Anonymous for me to
truly understand the differences between them.
Even though the contrasts are briefly covered in the
"Big Book" of Alcoholics Anonymous, it eluded me
for a number of years. Even at the professional level
I found its definition to be misunderstood.

I wanted also to include what to expect if you
decide to go to an AA meeting, in order to alleviate
some of the concern you may feel before you go to
one. It is my hope after reading this book you'll be
more comfortable going to a meeting to see if the
program and what it offers is for you.

Alcoholic or Problem Drinker?

The Difference between Alcoholism

and Problem Drinking

First, it's critical to know alcohol is a drug. Not only is it a drug, it is a narcotic drug. This means once taken to excess it becomes addictive. The same is true with many drugs, even nicotine. I remember watching TV the day the Surgeon General (just before he retired) stated that addiction to cigarettes was as powerful as heroin addiction. Boy, did that get the cigarette companies fuming. No pun intended.

The social uses of alcohol are obvious. It helps people to relax and socialize and there's nothing wrong with this. As mentioned earlier, the problem lies in its use when taken in excess. It is then the addictive properties come into play and the person can find themselves drinking more often, and even making drinking a priority over everything which can include family, job, and even their own health.

Alcoholism however is a different beast. It has symptoms that show itself as the disease it is. These have been expertly pointed out in A.A.'s Big Book which is available at most if not all meetings of Alcoholics Anonymous.

To name just a few of these symptoms, the first is that the alcoholic's perception of reality changes almost instantly with just a few drinks. The statement is "**the sense of ease and comfort that**

comes with a few drinks". It is a total change in how the person now views reality. Putting all things aside, an alternate reality now comes into play. This can happen in a small degree or to a total disregard for current reality.

This doesn't happen with social drinkers. Their reality stays the same. You'll hear them say things like, "well, time to go home, I have to work tomorrow" or worse, "my wife wants me home so we can go shopping later". We call these strange creatures "social drinkers".

The next symptom is the insidious one, the one that drive us to what is called "a pitiful and incomprehensible demoralization" of ourselves. It's important to know that the definition of the word insidious is perfect because it means "lying in wait", "to entrap", "treacherous, and cunning". This perfectly describes the disease of alcoholism.

One of the puzzling symptoms of alcoholism is known as "the insanity of that first drink". In spite of all evidence why a person should not take a drink, and there can be lots of very strong reasons not to drink, a truly ridiculous idea wins out over why it's okay to take a drink. It can come to the point where one considers their sanity is at stake.

However once alcohol is consumed, their so-called reasons for not drinking fall away and the person finds themselves drinking to extremes soon afterward. Even in spite of promises to themselves, family and friends, their drinking resumes to the same level of abandoning everything else. It's a very dangerous time for us when we have no effective mental defense against drinking.

Maybe you'll say to yourself, "I'll just have one drink and head right home or maybe drink wine instead of beer". Perhaps you might place a friend in charge of your drinking, (see how long that lasts) or worse, justify your return to serious drinking because someone made you angry and did you an injustice.

Alcoholism also has another revealing symptom, one that was my own tell-tale symptom. It was the Dr. Jekyll, Mr. Hyde syndrome. This manifests in many different ways with us.

Some drinkers become friendly and easygoing while drinking though they are normally tight lipped unfriendly, people. Alternatively, they may become dangerously belligerent or loudmouthed which is not their normal demeanor.

Others may break the law while under the influence of alcohol. This can include offenses like driving while impaired or other criminal acts such as violence to others. My disposition while drinking was friendly and sociable. I drank lots and rarely if ever became sick, however, during these periods of drinking I would break into places and rob the establishment, then wake up in the morning praying it was only a dream. It seemed like clockwork I would be in a jail cell just before something important was to happen. It happened again and again, but I never blamed my drinking. Why should I? I drank more than most, and I was quick to see the people who 'really had a problem', but I wasn't like them.

As an example, I once met a fellow while I was in Alberta. He was going to meetings for about a month when he said he asked to talk to me about something important. He said he realized the answer to staying sober lies within the recovery program in AA and he wanted it. He wanted it because he robbed banks when he drank. I don't know if he used a weapon but he said he became a different person when he drank. Now he saw the reality of AA's answer and knew if he wanted to stay sober and stop robbing banks, he had to get honest. He turned himself in that day and started his road to recovery.

Sure, that may seem to be extreme, but the torment felt by a person continually hurting themselves or the ones they love, feels the same. One lady I met in Ontario came to A.A because she was tired of waking up in the closet where she found herself after sobering up, going from one extreme emotion to another. The pain however, was the same.

The camps on alcoholism are divided as to whether there are three stages to the disease or four.

The first symptom of having the disease is that your perception of reality changes when you drink. You're comfortable in your own skin as A.A. likes to put it, not because you are slightly sedated by the drug but because now you are viewing your surroundings through a different perception. You may or may not be able to control your drinking at this stage, meaning you can go out "for a few" and be able to walk away without having to overindulge yourself, even though alcoholics generally have an amazing capacity to drink volumes of alcohol.

The second stage of alcoholism is the inability to stop drinking once you start. Simply put, once alcohol has been introduced to your body, craving starts and you must drink all you can get, and more.

The final stage, known as chronic, this is where you don't have to drink to be craving it. Once you wake or regain consciousness, you must have a drink to settle your nerves or stomach. Whatever the excuse may be, it is the final and most serious stage. Death usually comes soon after but not without a lot suffering to those afflicted and to those who care about the sufferer.

Problem Drinking

Problem drinking usually circles around the physical addiction to the drug alcohol. This can be broken or solved with treatment or some form of intercession like a doctor or family member. As stated in A.A.'s Big Book, "he may have the habit badly enough to impair him, or even cause him to die ahead of his time, but if a strong enough reason is given, he or she may be able to completely stop their drinking."

I met a fellow just like this!

I was mentoring a fellow around twenty-five years of age into recovery and while he was walking across a large street in Edmonton, he dropped to the ground and went into convulsions. Not a good place to drop to the ground with cars whizzing all around you! He was in good health otherwise, as most people are at that age except for this one deeply concerning episode.

He had been sober maybe three months or so at this time, so I located a doctor who knew of alcoholism (because it's best that a doctor knows about alcoholism in order to treat alcoholics) and advised him to get a full checkup. The outcome for the most part was that the episode was an alcoholic seizure. This sometimes happens to people when they stop drinking. He, the doctor, advised lots of water (because alcohol robs the body of fluids) and mixing the water with good sea salt for the mineral content and better eating which proved to be the solution.

Why sea salt? When you are dehydrated and go to a hospital you are usually given a saline IV drip. This is a mineral of sea salt! This can actually prevent DT's (delirium tremens) if given in time.

Anyways, what happened downstairs while I was waiting for my friend's examination by the doctor is what this story is really about.

While I was waiting in the lobby, an elderly gentleman named Barney was there, and he opened a conversation with me. Barney was a genuinely nice fellow. We started talking and it soon led up to the topic of his drinking. Essentially, his story was that he had started drinking in 1904, or somewhere around then, going into the bush with some friends to make cheap alcohol. They would get a twenty-gallon vat or barrel with water in it and put bran and yeast cakes in it to ferment. After twenty-four hours or so they would drink it, but it was so strong that they would actually lose their eyesight (!) and they would have to wait until it returned in order to find their way home. I forget how long he said he did this, but it was for a number of years.

Soon his drinking got him in trouble with the law, and he did some jail time. Later he did a stint in an insane asylum, and was in even more trouble with the law. He joined the army but was later discharged due to his drinking. This left him broke, but still he kept on drinking. Then, at the age of sixty-two, he went to a local Legion to drink, and after only a few drinks found himself home the next morning deathly ill. He said he was really afraid for his life and that he actually felt like he was going to die, so he went to his doctor and the doctor literally said to him, "Barney if you don't stop drinking, you're going to die".

He stopped then, and at the time we were talking it had been seven years since he had taken a drink.

At this point I had fire alarms going off in my head. What was the difference between Barney and me? He did all the things I had done and more yet here he was sober and seemingly fine with not drinking at all.

Now for one of the last symptoms of alcoholism, and it's a big one. The natural state of a SOBER alcoholic is irritable, restless, and discontented, maybe not right away but as time goes by, it gets worse. It took me only 4 years of living without a drink until I was at the point of wanting to commit suicide. This irritability presents itself in various ways but one of the common ones is that little issues cause inappropriate reactions while other times the large issues are glanced over as if it's not a big problem at all.

There's actually a joke I came across that seems to describe it perfectly. "An alcoholic doesn't mind if the milkman runs away with his wife, but he bloody well better leave the milk!"

This symptom is almost universal with addicts to all types of drugs, not just alcohol, even drugs like marijuana and nicotine. I have seen fits of rage taken out on spouses and children escalate in intensity as the amount of time away from these substances increases.

If you are simply a "problem drinker" all you need to do is stop drinking. You may need medical treatment such as a local detox facility to help you withdraw from the alcohol, but once you have some time sober you will be able to function as a person free from the addiction of alcohol.

Be aware however, if you should begin to see the signs of alcoholism mentioned earlier, as in irritability, restlessness, or even mental problems and not being able to sleep because of the 'voices' in your mind, being discontented with the way things are going, nothing is good enough, etc.,
If you are experiencing these problems, you may have the disease.

You see, with the addict/alcoholic, these drugs really are our solutions and what keeps us from going nuts a day at a time. You need to find another solution, one that can help you live sober successfully.

Hopefully this can give you a starting point of understanding the depth of the problem. If you're reading because a friend is in trouble with the bottle, there's not a lot you can do for him or her. You can let them know there is an answer and if they want, you can go to a meeting₁ with them so they're not alone. You can honestly say you want to see it for yourself, but don't be surprised if after the meeting they compare and point out differences instead of seeing how this can benefit them. Maybe they may ask if you'll go once again with them. There are some meetings just for men and some just for women. You can choose gender meetings if the person has issues around the opposite sex. It doesn't matter a lot, as long as they are exposed to the answer, a seed gets planted.

If you're reading this book for yourself, go to a meeting. Look one up online or grab your phone book and call. Do it now. You'll be glad you did, and so will those who care about you.

Waiting and putting it off can and will make things worse for you if you and alcohol are bad partners. That doesn't mean every time you drink there are problems, but sooner or later you'll have a bad turn of events escalating your problems significantly.

If you have alcoholism it will get worse. It's the nature of the beast so do something now, right now. Call, or look up a meeting in your phone book and go. Keep an open mind and listen to the speaker. If the message doesn't do anything for you, go to another because you're worth it. Besides, once you get better, the world around you seems to clean up its act a whole lot. Funny, but it's true.

Now let's see what science says…

What Science Has to Say About Alcoholism

Roughly thirty years ago one afternoon I turned on my television and happened upon an ongoing series known as The Nature of Things. This show was being hosted by internationally renowned Canadian scientist David Suzuki. To my surprise this particular documentary was about alcoholism.

I had just arrived home from an AA meeting which was being held in a local Alano Club$_2$ which many of the larger cities have that host AA meetings for Alcoholics. To arrive home after a meeting of Alcoholics Anonymous to find a scientist's research on this disease, one I respect very much, was a welcomed coincidence.

The documentary covered the research showing that alcoholism was an inherited disease and identified a particular gene in the DNA strand. He had concluded that without this particular gene a person would not have alcoholism. It **was not** to say that a person could not get addicted to alcohol, because anyone can, due to alcohol's addictive nature, but they could not drink themselves into alcoholism.

This statement seems to be backed up as well by the Big Book of Alcoholics Anonymous where it states the amount of alcohol an alcoholic drinks has nothing to do with it. In the Big Book of AA, in the chapter "More About Alcoholism" it reads:

"Several of our crowd, men of thirty or less, had been drinking only a few years, but they found themselves as helpless as those who had been drinking twenty years. To be gravely affected, one does not necessarily have to drink a long time nor take the quantities some of us have."

This statement identified me perfectly. I found myself entering AA at the age of twenty-four after several incidents with the law following my drinking.

I didn't get into trouble every time I drank but almost every time I had been in trouble, I had been drinking.

The documentary went further to say that the gene is not always dominant as it can skip generations. Your parents can have alcoholism and as their child you may or may not have the disease. If your grandparents had the disease you may find yourself showing the symptoms described earlier and show the signs of alcoholism soon if not immediately after drinking alcohol for the first time.

As with other diseases, periods of abstinence are not a curative measure. If you are an alcoholic, you cannot safely return to drinking after a period of sobriety. Diabetics, as an example, cannot return to a high sugar diet after having a sugar free program of eating for a number of years. It just doesn't work. The easiest way to help discern if you have alcoholism is to look for the symptoms of the disease.

You may be able to discover what stage of alcoholism you are in as well if you see that you have the symptoms, the first being a change in perception soon after drinking. Unlike social drinkers, your reality is now different than it was earlier and you may find yourself putting everything important aside to continue drinking.

The second stage is that you have great difficulty stopping drinking once you start, and then the final stage, needing to drink immediately upon awakening.

The confusion may arise when problem drinkers show these last two stages as well, however this is the addictive element of alcohol. Addiction treatment is still needed to break the physical addiction though they can resume a normal life after breaking the cycle of the addiction to alcohol.

The alcoholic, even though the addiction to the opiate of alcohol has been dealt with, will still return to drinking in spite of their knowledge that they must abstain. It is a baffling feature of this disease and Alcoholics Anonymous has found a way to stay sober one day at a time through the Twelve Steps of Alcoholics Anonymous.

Let's have a look at this program...

Alcoholics Anonymous

AA has its own preamble to every meeting. This is how it starts:

"Alcoholics Anonymous is a fellowship of men and women who share their experience, strength and hope with each other that they may solve their common problem and help others to recover from alcoholism".

Notice the portion of the sentence that says, "that they may solve their common problem *and* help others to recover from alcoholism"

It seems they are repeating themselves, but actually these are two separate issues a person with alcoholism faces. Recovering from their own alcoholism is number one if they have the disease of alcoholism, and solving their "common" problem, is number two.

The common problem is now living without alcohol as a solution.

Alcoholics Anonymous offers another solution that works better than any drug and this is to learn how to live using simple spiritual principals. Fortunately, these are easy to adopt and are not religious tenants or conditions at all. You don't have to believe, but just be *willing to believe* that there may be a greater power than your addiction that could help you stay clean and sober.

This simple principal has worked for millions of people to maintain contented sobriety. Many never return to drinking and enjoy productive, happy lives. Others take longer after returning to alcohol a few times but some eventually recover when they become willing to go to any length to get sober.

Tragically, there are also those who do not make it. They take their own lives being either unable or unwilling to live without alcohol. This happens far too often as there are many thousands affected by this deadly disease.

Let's take a look at what an AA meeting is.

What is an AA Meeting?

First, who can go to an A.A meeting?

Alcoholics Anonymous has two different formats for meetings. One is called a closed meeting and another, an open meeting.

A closed meeting is designed to only be for people who have a "desire" to stop drinking. Notice that I did not say they had to say they were alcoholics. This is because in one of the traditions of Alcoholics Anonymous to be a member of AA, you only have to have a "desire to stop drinking". It doesn't even mean you have to be sober when you go to a meeting. Some people are only able to go to a meeting with a shot or two under their belt. The *desire to stop* is the issue, the action can come later.

An "open meeting" is exactly that, open to anyone. If you would like to locate a meeting of AA, you can do a search on a local search engine like Yahoo or Google. Simply search for Alcoholics Anonymous meetings by typing "AA meetings" into the search bar followed by the name of your town.

If you don't have an internet connection, you can use your local phone book to find a meeting for that day.

Typically, AA meetings begin around 8:00 PM however, meetings can also run throughout the day. This usually depends on the size of the city, so if you're in a smaller city, you may find meetings will be only in the evening and these meetings generally run about one hour in length.

It's normal for people to show up half an hour in advance, and stay thirty minutes after the meeting to chat with friends and newcomers. It's also quite normal for people to show up five minutes before the meeting starts and leave right afterward. There are no rules for attendance.

Now, let's talk about what you can expect at a typical (open)$_3$ AA meeting.

What to Expect at a Meeting of Alcoholics Anonymous

As mentioned before, if you're trying to find a meeting of Alcoholics Anonymous in your area, just go to any search engine like Google and type in "AA meeting" for whatever your city is, and it will bring it right up.

Even if you're new to your city, when you're trying to find the meeting just look for a group of people standing outside having a cigarette or chatting and you'll know you're in the right place. It's not unusual to find some meetings are held in the basement or main floor of a church.

As you walk by this group of people, you can ask one of them privately, "Is this an AA meeting?" and they will let you know if you're in the right place or not. The person you asked may even take you in and show you where to get a cup of coffee or cup of tea. If you're woman, ask a woman. If you're man, ask a man.

Once inside, you may be introduced to people by the person who brought you in. If you're uncomfortable with that, just say so. Just ask for a place to sit and the person will be more than happy to accommodate you.

Keep in mind anonymity is a priority in our meetings, so if you see someone you recognize, do not worry, your identity is safe. That's why it's called "Anonymous".

Typically what happens then is that a person will come to the front podium and ask for the meeting to start. Alcoholics Anonymous will usually begin with a short prayer called the Serenity Prayer, a moment of silence, or both.

Then the person at the front will ask certain people to come up and read over different aspects of Alcoholics Anonymous. These can include the Twelve Steps, the Twelve Traditions, and something called "The Slogans". There may be some differences, but this is a general outline.

The slogans are simply short sentences or phrases each of us can use when we find ourselves in a tight spot. These are great little reminders to help us to stay focused and not become overwhelmed by life's upsets. You've probably even heard a few of them before.

A lot of meetings now also do something called 'The Chip System'. These "chips" are small medallions and are given out to people at various times of their sobriety during their first year. These can range from thirty days up to nine months however there is also one for the newcomer.

This chip is handed out to people who have a "desire to stop drinking" or have had at least one day without a drink. It is totally optional for you to pick this up if you want to stop drinking. If you have a problem with alcohol, this can be a good reminder why you came to the meeting in the first place.

You'll come across dozens of stories of people who found themselves at a bar, or going to a store to buy booze and they found these medallions in their pocket reminding them of their wish to try and stay sober. Sometimes it's enough of a reminder for these people to walk away from the temptation of starting to drink again.

If you're okay with getting a "chip" for your first day sober or you have a desire to be sober, you can go to the front when they offer it. You will simply be given the medallion with a handshake, and you can return to your seat. That's it. You won't be asked to speak at this meeting or say you're an alcoholic.

Once all of this is done, the person at the front will invite a person to come up and share their story. This has all been prepared before you came to the meeting, so no need to worry, you will not be asked to contribute. Besides, you need to listen more than you need to talk right now anyways. Don't you agree?

This next part is important.

The people who come to the front to share their stories are not professional speakers. They are simply people who are experiencing life without alcohol and wish to share their story with those who wish to listen, that's all. Sometimes however, their stories are more about alcohol, than living without alcohol. It just happens that way sometimes. As I said, these people are not professional speakers. They are just everyday people who are sharing their experience, strength and hope about their sobriety.

I will guarantee you however, eventually if you decide to visit more meetings, one day you will hear a speaker that will "knock your socks off". These types of speakers will tell their story in a simple way but their message will carry a powerful impact. These are the types of stories you need to hear. To know, no matter how far down you have gone, other people have gone as far or further and still found a way to a happy life. Once you hear a story that hits home, everything will change for you. To really know and believe you can live a happy, successful life is not only possible, but promised within the recovery program of Alcoholics Anonymous.

Once the meeting is completed, the person in charge of the meeting may close the meeting with prayer, or may not. It just depends if they do that in your area. Keep in mind, Alcoholics Anonymous meetings are not religious meetings, even though the word God may be said a lot during the course of the night. These meetings are based on spiritual principals and it's what we follow. We are not against churches or religion at all.

You'll soon recognize these are not the types of people you'll see in your local churches. But living spiritually is the key to successful, sober living.

Don't get me wrong, some of the members that to come to these meetings can be priests, police officers, lawyers, skid row bums, unemployed, and professional people. Each meeting will have a good cross-section of society in it. Only you won't know what they do for a living.

After the meeting is closed, you may be approached by people who either spoke, or saw you are new. This is normal. They simply wish to be helpful. If you found the meeting informative you can ask for a meeting list. Most groups will have one and they are free.

If the things the speaker talked about hit home with you, you can ask him or her for a phone number. Again, please stick to your own gender. It just avoids complications. You can even speak to other people in the meeting if you like, but you do not have to give out your own phone number. Feel free to ask for theirs though, but if you're going to ask for someone's phone number, use it. It may be an opportunity to get help when you really need it.

Lastly, if you have a problem with alcohol, go to more than one meeting. Give yourself the chance to hear what this program can provide and how you can use it to your own benefit. It will help those who care about you too if you decide to try living without alcohol or drugs.

Sometimes, if you're an attractive man or woman, you may be approached by someone of the opposite sex with seemingly good intentions. These intentions may be real and they may not be. Don't be surprised that this could happen at an AA meeting. It happens at lots of places where people gather, libraries, laundromats, churches and the work place. Just stay on track and stick to your gender, your sobriety will thank you later.

Also, you may be approached by someone who will try to "convince" you to come back, or that you're an alcoholic. This is against the teachings in our Big Book where it warns us more than once to never brand a person as an alcoholic. This is a determination that must be self-realized to have any real significance. This comes with learning about the disease and self-discovery.

Everything in this world has a good and bad side to it. Alcoholics Anonymous has its shortcomings just like any other organization, however you will soon recognize those who are *living the program*, so go to a meeting and listen to the speaker. Don't compare that person's actions to ones you may or may not have done. Just listen and see if this speaker has anything in his "talk" that may help you in any way.

I can promise you, in a short period of time it will be a life changing experience to the good. If you give it, or should I say yourself, a chance.

Now, a little about AA and the answer it holds...

How it Works

Does Alcoholics Anonymous hold the only answer
to the disease of alcoholism?

Yes and no.

Using the Twelve step program/process is a journey
to self-cleansing and learning to communicate, on a
one to one basis with a Power greater than
ourselves. This way you can live free from the
enemy of addiction and do so happily. AA is not a
self-help program. If we were able to help
ourselves, we wouldn't need a Higher Power.

There is a powerful transformation that can happen
to you, but it usually takes time depending on how
honest you are willing to be with yourself. People
can also use their personal faith in a religion of their
choice to face and be free from their chains as long
as they follow the same or similar guidelines to
achieve true sobriety.

We in AA certainly don't hold the only key to
successful sobriety. However, through years of
research and observation, I have never seen an
alcoholic find contented sobriety through anything
other than living with spiritual principals. Maybe it
will happen one day.

One of the definitions of sobriety I found that struck
home with me is "freedom from excess,
extravagance, or exaggeration".

The reason it struck a chord with me is because it first covered "excess" which drinking and drugging had certainly become in my life. "Extravagance", that was the big 'me', the great 'I am'. No one else really mattered, and my own grandiose ideas were all that concerned me. Alcoholics seem to be lovers of these grand ideas and will sometimes follow them, even the ridiculous ones, to our personal and sometimes our family's ruin. That's what my behaviors displayed. Then, ending with the term "exaggeration", which was a nailing down of my personal ego, this was the one thing that stood between me, my friends, family, God and even my own self-acceptance.

Let's see how this answer to the alcoholic dilemma was founded.

It was first discovered and made use of publicly in 1840 by an organization called the Washingtonian Movement. It was an incredible success as well. It started in Baltimore Maryland with six drunks who made pledges of total abstinence and even signed formal papers attesting to it. Within a year, the membership grew to over one thousand people and within the next three years it exploded to over four hundred thousand individuals staying sober each day.

The movement was based on the following six principles:

1. Each person would help one another.
2. Weekly meetings were attended.
3. Telling their story and the personal cleansing and changing of one's life.

4. Always to be available to others and members for help and fellowship.
5. Trusting God and living truthfully.
6. Total abstinence from alcohol.

History reveals within a few years the movement began to have issues with leadership, religious squabbles, and even some trying to make sobriety a professional business. You can't take a gift that was freely given and then charge others for it. It's a spiritual principal, the gift would have to be forfeited if you did.

Within eight years the Washingtonian Movement disappeared from society. Over four hundred thousand drunks lost their freedom from bondage.

But all was not lost...

Approximately eighty-seven years later another light in the darkness appeared and they were known as the Oxford Group.

They were far more religious in their tenets however, and their requirements to stay sober. They followed the same principles but these became rules and, in a sense, had to be strictly followed.

Problem is, rules don't fly with most drunks.

A few members from the Oxford Group knew this and devised another plan to help drunks get sober. Within a couple years they had around one hundred people living sober successfully and decided to tell the world. This came in the form of what is known today as "The Twelve Steps" and it was laid out in a book called "The Big Book of Alcoholics Anonymous."

About thirty years ago I was given the privilege of being shown around Alcoholics Anonymous' head office in New York by a wonderful woman who showed me some of their archives.

One of them that stood out was the first picture by the newspapers in New York of A.A. members. It was almost comical because each of the people in the picture were wearing a mask! They looked like bandits. However, A.A. was making real strides in helping people to find contented sobriety

and A.A.'s anonymity was critical in those days. No single person could represent the program should they falter and get drunk. This was so those who were considering joining AA wouldn't get discouraged thinking the program didn't work. It did work, and it worked very well for those who followed the steps as they were laid out. This was proven and still stands today. If you do the steps, you get better.

One of the documents shown to me was the original Twelve Steps just before they were about to be sent to press for printing. It was far different than what I knew from the Twelve Steps of today. It was different because the approach in the wording was stated as "you must" and "you admitted" and "you had to", not as it shows today with "We admitted" and "when we were wrong". I had a copy of it for many years but somehow lost it, or I would put it here so you could compare the two side by side. The differences were very stark at the time.

Changing the jargon was a key factor in helping egotistic, head strong people to have an open mind without having to be told what to do. It proved to be a winning formula, hands down.

In the beginning it was very different from today. I listened to a speaker who joined AA in those early days and he mentioned that when he wanted to stop drinking, he had to convince the person who came out to talk to him that he was serious. If this person believed him, he would be *allowed* to go to a meeting. First though, he would have to do steps 1, 2 and 3. *Then* he could go to a meeting. Immediately after the meeting he would have to start on the next step or he could not continue with AA.

This is why AA at the time showed a seventy-five percent recovery rate. It was a 'do it now or out you go' system. AA was far too important at the time to have people who just wanted to go to meetings but not do anything about their drinking. It worked and was available to those who wanted to use it.

I'm sure there were places that did not enforce the Twelve Steps like this in the beginning, but I certainly understand why this was done and how this organization grew with such a solid base for others to follow.

I'm going to end this book with my own story. You may see this as an extreme example of what people can go through but I have met others who have experienced even more than I have. It doesn't matter what you have gone through, you can get sober and even happy if you're willing to go to any length to get it.

My Story

It's important, even critical, to understand that telling your own story at an AA meeting is up to you. It won't happen until you've been around a few months or longer, but it's voluntary.

Telling your story is not about revealing your sins, or using the podium in a meeting as a confessional. That's not what this is about. You simply tell your story in a "general way" as the Big Book suggests.

Keep in mind as well that the things you say may 'trigger' people, as many adults have been victims of all kinds of horrific abuse. By telling our story in this general way, people focus more on the thoughts and feelings experienced by the teller, as opposed to situations this person has gone through. If you find my story difficult to continue reading, I apologize. I'll try to keep the descriptive details out as much as possible. All stories are different, this one is mine.

I've heard it said in meetings that most people can remember their first and/or their last drink. For the longest time I can't say I knew when my first drink was. Oddly enough though, a memory came to me while I was at a particular meeting of Alcoholics Anonymous about thirty years ago.

It was at this meeting a person made that statement, and in a flash, I went back in time to when I was a small boy. It was almost like a movie. We were living in Detroit where I grew up and I was standing at my father's bed. I still remember seeing that the top of the mattress came up to my stomach, so I must have been three or four years old. In this memory I see a glass of beer being offered to me to sip from, and when I took the sip, the foam went up my nose. The bubbles scratched as the beer coursed down my throat, then went 'boom' when it hit my stomach. I didn't like it, but I wanted more.

That memory had never revealed itself before but now it's like it happened yesterday. Even recalling that memory I can still sense the foam in my nose, the carbonation, and the explosion of alcohol when it landed. Even the conflicting thoughts and emotions are with me, those of not liking the sensations I felt taking that drink, yet wanting more. How could I have known what lay ahead in the years to come.

My mom ended up leaving my dad, which in those days was taboo. Keep in mind this is in the mid-to-late fifties and a single woman with children was scorned. She decided to put us in foster care which was about the only thing that was available to her, so I spent the next year and a half with people I didn't know. This must have been a terrible time for her because I know that she loved us very much.

Then one day I was introduced to my new stepfather. Because I'd blanked out most memories, it wasn't until many years later I found out he was an abuser of the worst kind.

I was told many years later that I was breaking all the toys he gave me, so he told my mom I was disruptive to the household and needed to go back to foster care. She saw my behaviors but didn't know what was causing them, so she agreed. He threatened to leave if I wasn't removed from the home. This would have terrified her as she would have to start all over again so off I went into children services.

When a child is told he was being taken from his home because he is a bad boy, he will act out as a bad boy. Every home I went to I caused trouble. I stole, I ran away, I even made the occasional fires. Fortunately, no one was injured, but I kept moving from one foster home to another, then to institutions, and on to a reform school.

The reform school I was sent to had a secret. The "Christian" brothers who oversaw it were torturing and molesting thousands of kids over a twenty-year period. The police and other authorities were aware of what was going on but were afraid to try to accuse the Catholic Church openly. Finally, after 20 years of reports about this abuse, it came out into the open and charges were laid against the people involved.

Needless to say, coming out of that situation, I was pretty screwed up. I was an angry kid who didn't want to talk to anyone, and who didn't want to be close to anyone, understandably so.

I think I was 15 when I got out of reform school and for the next three years or so my behaviors continued, however, now I was beginning to be exposed to something different, nice people and a new creature, ...girls! If you can imagine a young fellow, having been in institutions and foster homes for most of his life, he would have few to no social skills. This certainly was the case with me. I didn't have a clue how to communicate with people, but something interesting happened. I realized that I loved to listen to people who would talk with me.

I remember the first conversation I ever had on the telephone. Someone had called just to talk to me! This was the very first time I talked on the phone in a personal and private conversation. I remember loving the conversation, laughing at all the things he was saying, and clarifying the points he was trying to make while he was on the phone with me. It was such an enjoyable experience for me that I remember it to this day.

Even the fellow who I was talking with, and I don't remember who this person was, commented how much he enjoyed our conversation, even though he did all or most of the talking. But my excited participation made that conversation a lot of fun for both of us.

All throughout those years I was in different foster homes, my mother never contacted me or wrote me letters and neither did any of my other family members. I don't blame her now, but I held resentments about it for a long time until the Twelve Step process removed them.

Talking to anyone before this was usually a result of being questioned about something I had done, and that usually inspired only lies. Now I have people genuinely interested in talking to me. This was awesome! I became a great conversationalist and used it to get attention, but even if I was in a crowd, I always felt as if I were alone. I just couldn't shake that feeling.

In high school while in grade 9, a fellow offered me a small piece of paper and called it blotter acid. Little known to me, this was LSD, a narcotic drug. He didn't tell me anything about what this thing really was, only I would probably really like it, so one day while we were taking exams, I decided to take this piece of paper to see if it would help me do better with my exams. It didn't. Within three hours I had left the school and was making my way through a swamp trying to avoid a police car I had seen out on the highway when I'd left the building. This was my introduction to paranoia.

I continued to take harmful chemical drugs and within a couple of years, I was lying in a sanatorium in a coma that lasted almost three months. I never knew I was in a coma until about six or seven years later when I was talking to my mom and mentioned I went to the hospital for the weekend. She looked at me kind of strange and said "you were there for three months".

I remember when I came around, one of the sanitarium workers showed me a couple young boys who were both in a constant state of seizure and were each plugged into some sort of machine just to keep them alive. If I remember right, he said they were around twenty-one and were just starting puberty. He also said they weren't going anywhere. Honestly, I can say I really didn't understand his point. I was just a kid, not to mention I was coming out of a three-month coma, so I think it's safe to say I wasn't very lucid. In any event, I went back home and decided I didn't want to do drugs anymore. I didn't for almost two years, but then I did them one more time and had a really bad trip. Thank God I survived it because it was such a bad experience, I didn't think I would. It really was that bad.

For some reason I didn't start drinking until I was 18, it was the legal age to drink back then but something very special for me happened when I started drinking. The nervousness I'd always felt inside went away almost instantly! It wasn't until years later into my sobriety I was able to see it as one of the symptoms of the disease. This was the altered perception of reality I spoke of earlier, it instantly changed once I took a drink. I was comfortable in my own skin for the first time that I could remember.

I loved it. I felt alive and didn't feel alone anymore! For the first time in my life I felt equal with everyone around me. It was like everybody was the same, no one was better than me or less than me. We were all equal and the women were no longer a threat to talk with. If I walked up to a lady and asked her to dance and she turned me down, so what, it was her loss. I just wanted to dance. I was okay with being turned down, and I shrugged it off with no problem at all. Alcohol had become a solution for me.

The bad side of it was, I also had no problem getting into fights with people and some of these people I had no business fighting with. Once, I got into a fight with the Golden Gloves boxer that must have lasted twenty minutes. I was so drunk I never even hit him, but he hit me plenty of times. Maybe this is one of the times alcohol helped me because I didn't feel a single punch.

The next morning I had exams at school. Exams were held in the auditorium so there were about three hundred kids there. I remember when I walked into the room everyone turned around to look at me. I was a mess with two black eyes, multiple contusions with all kinds of cuts on my face. I looked like I had performed mouth to mouth on a lawn mower set to mulch.

The girl I'd been defending in this fight came up to me, yes it was over a girl, asking me if her boyfriend had done this. I just said I had accidentally fallen off the back of a pickup truck, which she didn't believe, but I swore to myself I would get back at this guy and really clean his clock. Thankfully, I never had that opportunity. No one wants to go through something like that twice. It was my ego that was as badly bruised as my face.

I mentioned earlier something interesting had happened as I became a little older. I began to enjoy my freedom. I enjoyed walking around with no one telling me what to do. After twelve years in foster homes, institutions, jails and reform schools, freedom was an incredible experience. But alcohol had different plans for me.

When I drank, I became a different person and stupid ideas seemed brilliant. I began to break into establishments and relieve them of the money they made. Then I would wake up in the morning, finding hundreds or thousands of dollars on the bed beside me. Honestly, I was in shock because I knew this could put me back in jail and I didn't want to go back there.

Oddly enough, I never put two and two together. I never once considered alcohol played a part in this problem. I have since learned alcoholism blinds the sufferer to the disease. This way it's everybody else's fault, not the drinker's.

It was only a matter of time before I was in front of a judge on serious charges, but alcoholics seem to have a way to talk themselves out of almost anything, and I was a great talker. I convinced that Judge to let me go, and he did. However, he gave me a warning. He said if he ever saw me again, I could guarantee myself a long vacation. I actually went to the judge's chambers later to shake his hand I wanted to congratulate him on making a great decision. I really was convinced I wouldn't get into trouble anymore as I had promised myself and him, I would behave.

Little did I know I was powerless over alcohol. Once it was in me, I could not guarantee my behaviors. This was another lesson I'd have to learn the hard way. Six months later I was back in front of that same judge for breaking into a person's home.

I had no idea that in Canada, breaking into a home is punishable up to a maximum of 20 years! Small time jails and institutions are now being put aside in favor of penitentiary time and the penitentiary is a whole different world.

While I was in jail waiting for my sentence to be determined, a fellow in the cell next to me had been given five years. He was about twenty to twenty-five years old, and a good-looking guy. One day a huge fellow (and I do mean huge!) was standing outside his cell throwing kisses at him. He was saying to him that when he got to the penitentiary, come and look him up. If he didn't, everyone else would get him and he would wind up with him afterward, so he said to save himself a lot of trouble, come to see him and avoid the problem. He would protect him and he would be his boy.

I couldn't imagine what was happening in that next cell, but I knew what was going on in mine. This wasn't going to happen to me anymore. That night I attempted to end my life by hanging myself with the bed sheets in the cell. I failed. The next morning I woke up with sore protruding eyes from the attempted hanging, and a splitting headache.

I think this was when I hit my bottom. AA calls it a "pitiful and incomprehensible demoralization." It's a bottom I wouldn't wish on anyone, but almost everyone in AA knows what this is about and how it feels. I surrendered to the idea I needed to be put away. Maybe this way I would stop hurting the people I loved. Little did I know my surrender was the key that would introduce a change in my approaching destiny.

Then something happened, and it was a very unusual situation because it didn't make sense. You need to understand the scenario here. I'm facing a life sentence which, in the very least, means I'm going to the penitentiary, and just attempted suicide the night before. I remember a guard came around and asked if anyone wanted to talk to a fellow from AA. I had no idea what AA was, or even what it

stood for and besides that, I was feeling sociable(?).
That's what really strikes me today. What made me
want to talk to a stranger about something I didn't
understand after I had experienced the worst night
of my life? It just didn't make sense but thank God I
did talk to him.

All I remember about this guy is he was genuine.
He told me some stories about his drinking and the
problems he got into. Most of them were pretty
funny, and I enjoyed the conversation we had.

Looking back now I'm pretty sure he understood I
had no idea what my problem was. I'm certain
because he asked me to do something very unusual.
He asked me to think about the different times I had
been in trouble when I got back to my cell to see if
there was a coincidence. I remember wondering
why he would ask me such a ridiculous thing, but I
really liked the guy, so I promised I would.

Later that night, sitting in that dark jail cell I
realized either all or most of the time I've gotten
into trouble, I was drinking. It was almost as if
someone had lit a match in a totally dark room.
Everything was now crystal clear.

You see, I was convinced I had to be mentally
insane. It was the only thing that made sense to me.
I was tired of hurting people I cared about. I was
tired of being an embarrassment to my family, and I
just didn't want to live anymore. But no matter how
much I promised myself, I kept getting into trouble.
This new revelation suggested maybe I wasn't
crazy. Maybe I have this thing he talked about
called alcoholism, but how do I contact him again?

The next day I asked the guard how to meet this guy again or when he would come back and the guard said he had no idea who this fellow was nor if he even would come back again. Man, …that was frightening. The thought of some guy possibly having the answer to the biggest dilemma of my life, and maybe never seeing him again scared me to my very core. I desperately needed to talk to this guy again.

Fortunately, he showed up a few days later. I remember talking to him and wondering if I had this thing he called alcoholism. He said I might but I would need to go to some meetings to find out. I remember saying to him, "but I'm going to sentenced soon!". He just looked at me and said, "Do you want to get sober or just get out of jail?"

I realized if I could find a solution to my problem maybe I could put jail behind me. So I told him I just wanted to find out if I had alcoholism. He smiled and told me what I needed to say to the judge. Basically, this is what he said. "Don't try to be smart and come up with some stories to con the judge. There are a lot of people smarter than you, and they're still in jail. Just tell the judge you found out you may be an alcoholic, and wherever he decides to send you, could it please be a place where you can learn about alcoholism. That's it."

I still remember that day standing in front of that Judge, the same judge who said he was going to send me on a long vacation if he ever saw me again. Here I am again six months later, standing in a prisoner's box. I recited the lines my new friend had told me. I could barely stand up because my knees were shaking so badly, but I wanted to be honest. I was watching the pen he had in his hand and it looked like he had written a 7 on his paper, then scratched it out and wrote what looked to be a 5. He looked up at me and said," I don't know why, but I'm going to give you another chance."

If you've been in trouble with the police a few times there's a good chance you have a police officer who knows you by your first name. Well I had one too. He was standing off to my right and he was all excited because he finally had me cold, when the judge said he was going to give me another chance, I heard him say a word I don't want to repeat. He was furious. This guy had been focused on busting me for a few years and now I was getting another chance.

I remember a year before this, meeting him on the street a couple of days just after Christmas. He walked around the corner and almost walked right into me. I was surprised, but I stuck out my hand and said "Merry Christmas." He shook mine and said Merry Christmas to me as well. I asked him, "Has Santa been good to you?" He looked at me and said "No" so I asked why. He leaned forward and looked me right in the eye and said "cause I didn't get you!" That's how much he wanted to bust me. A year later, almost to the day, I was in the city jail cell after he had arrested me.

One night, he came to the cell and unlocked the door and said to follow him to interrogation. He walked in front of me by a couple feet, and I saw the gun in his holster. I thought for a second, grab the gun, shoot this guy, and then shoot myself. Really, I was in that kind of state.

But all of a sudden I realized this guy wasn't stupid, so I didn't try it. When I got into the room, I asked him what the big idea was, walking in front of me with his gun. He looked at me and smiled and said "It's not loaded, but I was hoping you'd go for it." That's how badly he wanted me.

Then I was standing in front of the judge, this officer had finally got me, and the judge was saying he'd give me one more chance? Honestly though, when this cop got angry, I didn't care. Something incredible was happening. Little did I know it was the beginning of a whole new life for me.

That day, the sentence given to me was ninety days in a camp for alcoholics. I was in shock, but I was grateful. I remember going to this camp and genuinely wanting to know if I had this thing, they called alcoholism. I would not drink, or take any drugs, while I was in this camp. (If you are not aware of it, drugs and alcohol are available anywhere, even in jails.)

I found another fellow there, a young native man who felt the same way I did. He wanted to see if he was an alcoholic. We became close friends during those 90 days and we both worked hard to stay sober. Each Friday night at the camp, a few people drove in to share their stories at our AA meeting. It was on the first night these people visited our camp someone told my story. (What this means is, this person went through many of the same things I did and his experiences were almost identical - *in a general way* - and it just floored me). Someone else went through what I was just coming out of. It was an amazing experience. It happens to many people, hearing someone has gone through almost identical situations. I have heard my story told twice in all the time I have spent in AA so far, both that night, and about a year ago at a meeting where I live today.

At the end of ninety days I believed alcohol was the issue, so I could still smoke pot. It didn't work.

I heard later that switching addictions is like changing seats on the Titanic. You're still going down!

Within a short time I was irritable over stupid little things and I was hurting people I loved again. At my wits end I considered ending my life. I pictured myself jumping off my twenty-story building, but as I pictured myself falling, I changed my mind. In reality however, that wouldn't matter, you'd just keep falling.

(My son, being a typical teenage comedian, commented once said that a lot of people who jump off buildings die before they think they will. It's because they don't factor in the thirteenth floor.

Kids...)

In any event, I knew I didn't want to die. I just didn't want to go on living the way I was so I called AA. Fortunately, when I got through, a person listened to me and said I just needed to get to a meeting and everything would be okay. I was still suffering from alcoholism. I told him I wasn't drinking anymore, but he just said to me, you can suffer from alcoholism sober too. That really struck at me, but I was excited because he also said I was going to be okay and I headed off to my first meeting in sobriety.

I would like to tell you I jumped in with both feet and took advantage of what this program could do for me but that was not the case. For the next four years I floundered around in AA going from meeting to meeting, learning how to talk the AA way and even get along with its members. I tried to clean up my act by not lying, I stopped stealing, and even worked on being a better person. Problem is, if you're an alcoholic, this won't work. A spiritual experience is what's needed, not a promise to behave. It's part of that unmanageability thing.

One day at the end of these four years I had realized that without even thinking, I had stolen an item from a store I was in. With my prior record I would have instantly gone to jail and if convicted, a lengthy prison term would have been given because of my prior record.

I was terrified. What happened to my resolve? I was sober, and without thinking at all I placed my freedom in jeopardy!

At that moment I realized the only thing I was doing in AA was "hanging around". I did not do the steps at all. I just learned how to talk about them, that's it.

So right there I became determined to do the Twelve Steps and if they didn't "work" for me there was no point to continue.

It was that day I found my first sponsor, a man who would mentor me through the Twelve Step program for the next five years.

We began the Twelve Steps within a couple of days and although I wasn't sure what I was doing, I trusted this person more than I had ever trusted anyone in my life. He was an amazing man. I even wound up putting him on a pedestal which I don't recommend you do, because it just creates problems. I had never really understood what the Twelve Steps meant until I actually worked them for myself.

I was literally transformed. A part of me within 'woke up' and I seemed to be able to live in a harmonious state without alcohol. It was fleeting at times as life consistently throws curves at us, but when I applied the principals, it worked!

There's a movie with Jeff Bridges where he survives an airplane crash and comes out of it in a euphoric state. When someone tried to get him to lie about the accident (for insurance reasons) it causes him to 'flip out' because it threatened his peaceful state. But he finds his own way to get his euphoric feelings back so he can live in peace with himself and his surroundings.

This is very similar within the AA program as one of the core principals is to practice "rigorous honesty". This is far more than just basic honesty. It's working to ensure every aspect of your life is aboveboard, to be able to go to bed at night with the approval of your own conscience. Before you can live this way however, you have to clean up the past, or you'll never be able to do it.

The Twelve Steps can be done every few years to help keep you "in tune" spiritually as you will discover more and more about yourself as your journey continues. You'll find deeper and deeper truths about yourself and life will astound you. Your life, and that of your family and friends will change for the better. Sometimes you will lose friends because they are not willing to be around someone who doesn't drink or partake in any other drugs than alcohol. That's normal, and if you stay on track, you may be able to help them in the future if they should ever show up at a meeting.

Only because of the Twelve Steps and it's transformative effects in my life, I have become a good father and a far better person than I ever hoped to be. I still screw up once in a while, but I have tools that work (when I use them) to put me back into a harmonious way of living. All I have to do is 'do it' and the action starts the answer working for me.

If you and alcohol are a bad mix, keep this last important fact in your mind.

It will get worse. It always does. Just look at your behaviors two or three years ago and compare those with now. You should see your behaviors getting worse. Do something about it today, while you can. Things can only get better if you apply the program to your life. Besides, consider the alternative...

I wish you the best my friend.

Anonymous Guest

Recommended Books

The Big Book of Alcoholics Anonymous

The 12 Traditions of Alcoholics Anonymous

A New Pair of Glasses: by Chuck C.

Mr. God This is Anna

Drop the Rock: Removing Character Defects –
Steps 6 & 7

Other Books by Anonymous Guest

All 12 Steps of Alcoholics Anonymous Explained
in Today's language

Each Step of Alcoholics Anonymous (one at a time)

How to be an Effective Sponsor in Alcoholics
Anonymous

Manufactured by Amazon.ca
Bolton, ON

37725282R00032